Transport AROUND THE WORLD

Boats and Ships

Chris Oxlade

Heinemann LIBRARY

www.heinemann.co.uk
Visit our website to find out more information about Heinemann Library books.

To order:
 Phone 44 (0) 1865 888066
 Send a fax to 44 (0) 1865 314091
 Visit the Heinemann Bookshop at www.heinemann.co.uk to browse our catalogue and order online.

First published in Great Britain by Heinemann Library, Halley Court, Jordan Hill, Oxford OX2 8EJ a division of Reed Educational and Professional Publishing Ltd.
Heinemann is a registered trademark of Reed Educational & Professional Publishing Ltd.

OXFORD MELBOURNE AUCKLAND
JOHANNESBURG BLANTYRE GABORONE
IBADAN PORTSMOUTH (NH) USA CHICAGO

Designed by Paul Davies
Originated by Ambassador Litho Ltd
Printed in Hong Kong/China

04 03 02 01 00
10 9 8 7 6 5 4 3 2 1

ISBN 0 431 10841 2

British Library Cataloguing in Publication Data

Oxlade, Chris
    Boats and ships. – (Transport around the world)
    1.Ships – Juvenile literature 2.Boats and boating –
    Juvenile literature
    I.Title
    623.8'2

Acknowledgements
The Publishers would like to thank the following for permission to reproduce photographs: Phil Thomas p8; Corbis: Neil Rabinowitz p5, Joel W Rogers p6, p9, Dave G Houser p14, p16, Carl Purcell pp19, 29; Quadrant Picture Library: Graham Laughton p4, Mike Nicholson p12, p20, p21; The Stock Market: Tom Stewart; Tony Stone Images: Gordon Fisher p10, Tony Craddock p11, David H Endersbee p17, Vince Streano p22, Sylvain Grandadam p23, John Lund p24, Ian Murphy p25, Oli Tennent p26, James Bareham p27, Robin Smith p28; Trip: H Rogers pp7, 18, M Garrett p15

Cover photograph reproduced with permission of Tony Stone

Every effort has been made to contact copyright holders of any material reproduced in this book. Any omissions will be rectified in subsequent printings if notice is given to the Publisher.

Contents

Any words appearing in the text in bold, **like this**, are explained in the glossary.

What is a boat?

A boat is a small craft that floats on water. People use boats for fishing, for travelling and for fun. Ships are bigger than boats. They are mainly used for transport.

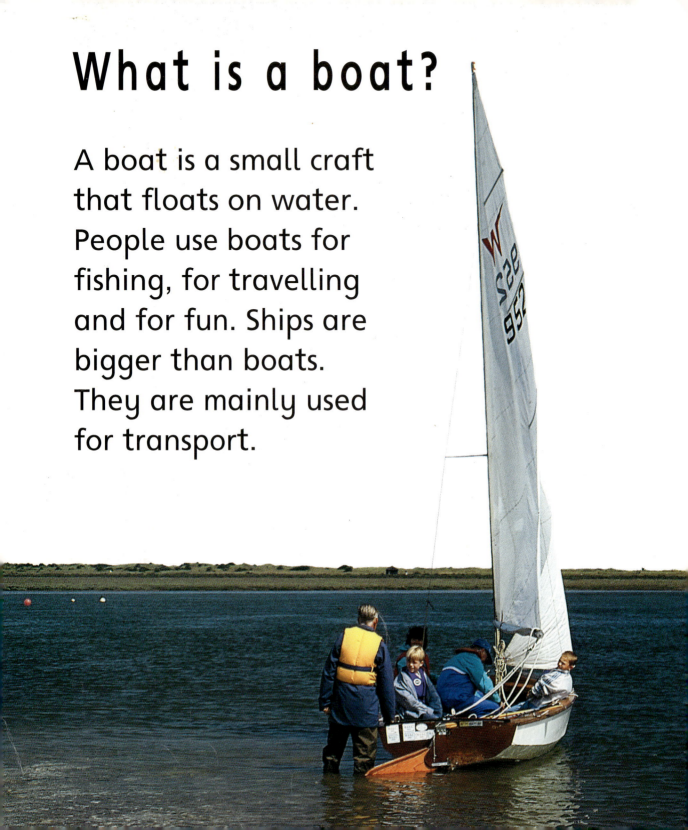

All ships have a **crew** of sailors. They **steer** the ship and work its machinery. The captain is the person in charge of the ship and its crew.

How boats work

Some small boats, such as this kayak, are moved along with paddles. The paddler also uses the paddle to **steer** to the left or right.

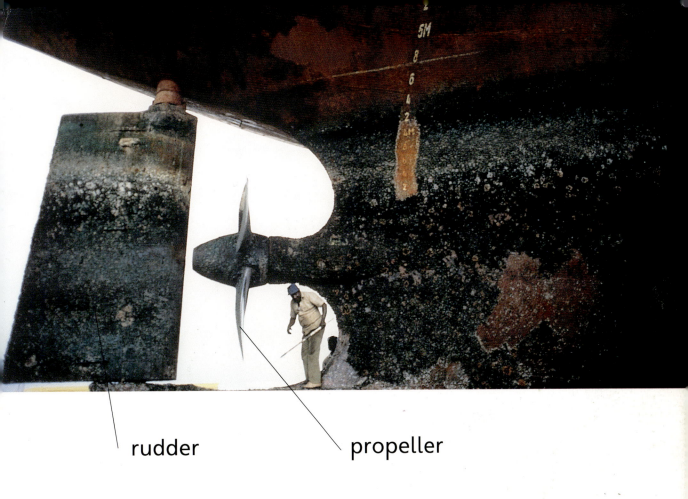

rudder   propeller

Larger boats and ships have an **engine** that turns a **propeller**. The propeller pushes the boat through the water. A **rudder** steers the boat to the left or to the right.

First boats

This wooden boat is called a long boat. People called Vikings built boats like this about a thousand years ago. They had oars and some had a square sail too.

This steamship was called *Leviathan*. It was built about 150 years ago. Passengers travelled in it across the Atlantic Ocean between Europe and America.

Where are boats used?

Ships and large boats travel from one **port** to another across the sea. They often have to sail through stormy weather and large waves.

Some boats do not go to sea. They only travel on rivers, lakes and **canals**. This wide, flat **barge** is carrying **cargo** along a river.

Fishing boats

Every day, fishermen go out to sea in their fishing boats to try to catch fish. Some fishing boats stay at sea for many days or even weeks.

Large nets are used to catch the fish.
The fishermen throw the nets into the
sea. The boat pulls them along behind it
and traps the fish. These men are sorting
out their catch.

Gondolas

In Venice in Italy, there are **canals** instead of streets. People use boats called gondolas instead of taxis to get around the city.

The person who sails a gondola is called a gondolier. The gondolier stands up and uses a very long pole to move and **steer** the gondola.

Ferries

A ferry is a ship that carries cars, trucks, buses and passengers. The vehicles are parked on **decks** inside the ship. Passengers sit on the upper decks.

There is a huge door in the ferry's **bow**.
It opens to let vehicles drive on and off.
This type of ferry is called a roll-on,
roll-off ferry.

Hydrofoils

A hydrofoil is a very fast type of boat.
It is often used to carry passengers.
Hydrofoils zoom along with their **hulls**
out of the water.

18

On the bottom of the hydrofoil's hull are small wings called foils. As the hydrofoil speeds up the foils lift it out of the water.

Aircraft carriers

An aircraft carrier is a type of ship used by a navy. It is like an airfield at sea. Planes can take-off and land on its huge **deck**.

A catapult gives planes a push so they
can go fast enough to take-off. When
the planes land, they are stopped by a
strong wire stretched across the deck.

Sailing

A junk is a sailing ship used in China for moving **cargo**. When the wind blows, it pushes on the sails, making the junk move along.

mast

amboo pole

The junk's sails are made of cloth.
Bamboo poles sewn to the sails make
them stiff. Tall, wooden posts called
masts hold up the sails.

23

Container ships

Containers are metal boxes that are filled with different sorts of goods or **cargo**. A container ship carries hundreds of containers in its **hold** and on its **deck**.

At a **port**, huge cranes load containers on to the ship. The containers arrive at the port on trucks and railway wagons.

Power boats

A power boat is a small, fast boat used for racing. Power boats have very powerful **engines**. They skim across the surface of the water.

When the sea is rough a power boat jumps from wave to wave. The **crew** have a very bumpy ride, so they must wear seat belts and crash helmets.

Cruise liners

A cruise liner is a ship on which people spend their holidays. On the ship there are restaurants, shops, swimming pools and rooms called cabins for passengers.

A cruise liner carries small boats called lifeboats. In an emergency the passengers and **crew** climb into the lifeboats and are lowered safely into the sea.

Timeline

3500 BCE The Ancient Egyptians build sailing ships with square sails and oars. They are the first sailing ships that we know about.

1000 CE The Viking people of Northern Europe build strong wooden long boats. They make long journeys across the seas to fight and trade.

1519 The Portuguese explorer Ferdinand Magellan and **crew** set out from Europe. One of his ships sails completely around the world.

1620 Dutchman Cornelis Drebbel builds the world's first submarine. It is a rowing boat covered with leather to keep out the water.

1808 A boat called the *Clermont* carries passengers along rivers in the USA. It is the first boat powered by a steam **engine**.

1912 The passenger liner *Titanic* sinks after hitting an iceberg in the Atlantic Ocean. More than 1500 people lose their lives.

1959 The first hovercraft is tested. It is called the *SR-N1*.

Glossary

barge	a long flat boat
bow	the front of a boat or ship
canal	a deep, wide ditch filled with water that boats and ships can sail along
cargo	goods carried on a ship
crew	the people who work on the boat or ship
deck	a flat floor on the top of or inside a boat
engine	a machine that powers movement using fuel. A ship's engine moves the ship along.
hold	the part of the ship where cargo is stored
hull	the main part of a boat or ship. The hull sits in the water.
port	a place on the coast or on a large river where ships go to load and unload their cargo
propeller	the part of the boat that spins round and moves the boat forward
rudder	the part of the boat that is used to steer
steer	to guide the direction of the boat or ship
stern	the back of a boat or ship

Index